Christianity

This book belongs to

PEGASUS

www.pegasusforkids.com

Published by Kuldeep Jain for B. Jain Publishers (P) Ltd., D-157, Sector 63, Noida - 201307, U.P

Printed in India

This graded series is written in easy-to-understand English. The aim is to develop reading habit in children and to increase their vocabulary.

Christianity is one of the most popular religions in the world. People who follow Christianity are called Christians.

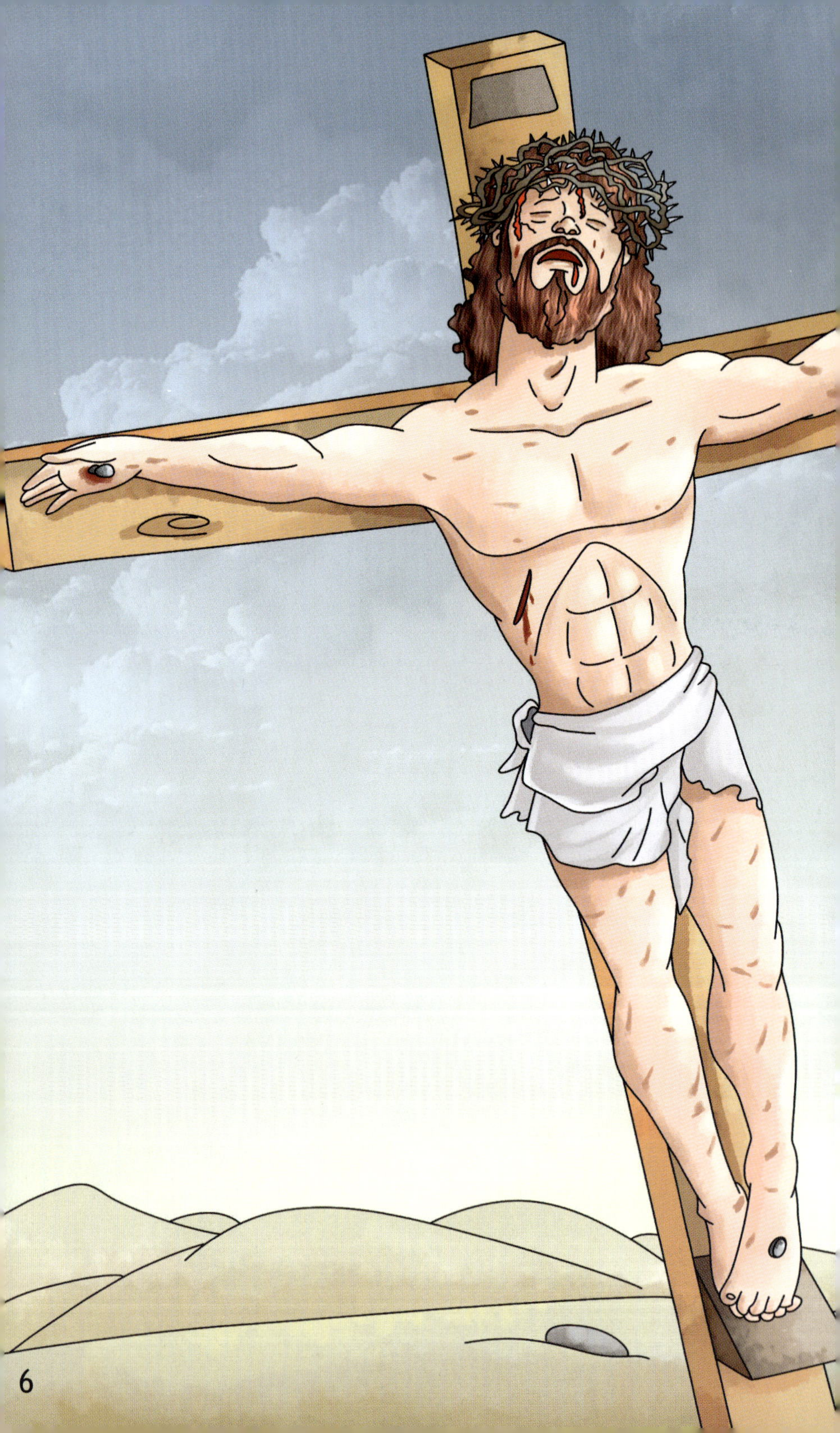

The holy book of Christians is called the Bible. Christians follow the teachings of Jesus Christ. Jesus Christ is believed to be the son of God. Christians believe God sent Jesus Christ on Earth to save humankind from sins and evil.

Jesus was born in a stable in Bethlehem in sixth century BC. Jesus was born to Joseph, a carpenter, and his wife, Mary.

Everyone heard of this miracle birth. Jesus' birth was seen as a threat by Herod the Great, who was emperor of Judea. Herod ordered that all male children in Bethleham, under the age of two be killed.

But an angel warned Joseph about this cruel order. Joseph took Mary and little Jesus to Egypt and hid there. Once Herod died, Joseph, Mary and Jesus returned and settled in Nazareth.

Jesus's true role began after he turned 30. That was when he began to spread the word of God. Jesus is believed to have gone into the Judean desert to meditate for 40 days and 40 nights.

On his return, he performed his first miracle of turning water into wine at a wedding. Soon, Jesus and his 12 disciples began spreading the word of God. But his fame worried the high priests.

So, Judas, one of Jesus's disciples, betrayed him for 30 piece of silver to the authorities. Judas told the high priests and Roman authorities where Jesus was. They arrested Jesus after the Last Supper.

The next day, Jesus was taken to the court where he was beaten for claiming to be the Son of God. Jesus was then nailed to a cross and crucified (crucifixion). He was buried in a nearby tomb.

But three days later, Jesus rose from the dead (resurrection). He appreared before his disciples and asked them to spread the word of God. Forty days after rising from the dead, Jesus went into Heaven.

Jesus's disciples then spread the word of God. Jesus's teaching were put together in the form of stories, parables, etc. in the Holy Bible.

Jesus's birth, crucifixion and resurrection are important dates for Christians.

His birth is celebrated as Christmas, his crucifixion is observed as Good Friday and his resurrection is celebrated as Easter.

One of the main customs in Christianity is baptism. This custom is conducted to remove sin and accept Christianity as the faith. These baptisms are performed by Christian spiritual heads called priests or ministers.

Christians pray in churches. The Holy Cross is accepted by all as the common symbol of Christianity.

New Words To Learn

miracle	authorities
emperor	parables
meditate	baptism
fame	crucifixion
betrayed	resurrection